JUST PRAY THE WORD

VOLUME 1

by

Pamela W. Roberts

ISBN: 9781521844588

Kindle Direct Publishing

Table of Contents

Introduction

Even though I walk through the [sunless] valley of deep darkness, I will fear no evil, for You are with me; Your rod [to protect] and Your staff [to guide], they comfort and console me. Psalm 23:4 (AMP)

Why LORD? Why me?

Why sickness?

Why financial difficulties?

Why divorce?

Why death?

Why loneliness?

Why disappointment?

Why distress?

Why me LORD?

During some of my dark valley walks in life, I have asked God, friends and myself these same questions. With tear filled eyes, I have sat in my room wondering if I would make it through the night. It sometimes seemed as if my difficulties were an endless cycle that never stopped. My Heavenly Father answered each one of my questions and He answered them every time I asked. The problem was I was not really listening. When God answered my questions with, "Because I want you to trust Me more", I did not want to accept that answer. I wanted my pain and troubles to go away. I am continuously learning more, through each trial and difficulty I experience, that trials and difficulties are the very things that draw me closer to God.

God is Creator, Ruler and Controller of EVERYTHING. He uses our past trials to remind us how He brought us through. God uses the present trials in our lives to increase our faith and trust in Him. God, our heavenly Father, will use our future trials to ensure us when they come, He will step in again as before. God's record is good! God wants to make us more like His Son, Jesus Christ, our Savior and the Ultimate Earthly Example.

That is exactly what my trials did for me. Of course, my flesh and feelings did not like it. It definitely did not feel good at all. The heartache, the distress, the pain, and the many tears I shed were almost too much for me to bear. OOOO--- but PRAISE GOD, what hurts the flesh, helps and heals the soul! You see, I have learned that this world and my flesh are temporary, but Heaven and my soul are eternal.

One of the difficult times in my life was in 2013. As my marriage began to really show signs of deterioration, the one and only company I had ever worked for in my career from college (25+ years) announced they were closing their doors and leaving the city. As life's crises were weighing heavy on me, I began to meditate more on God's Word and His Promises. There is power in the Word of God. Hebrews 4:12 says, *For the word of God is living and powerful, and sharper than any two-edged sword, piercing even to the division of soul and spirit, and of joints and marrow, and is a discerner of the thoughts and intents of the heart.* (NKJV) As I read more and meditated more, I grew deeper in the Word and realized that if the Word has Power, me praying the Word must also have Power. What a great concept from God.

As I continued spending time in God's Word, His promises to His people, I began writing and praying these promises back to Him. That is when my focus began to move from my trials to my triumphs in God.

Satan continued to tempt me with doubt, fear and frustration, but God's Word gave me strength and power to go on. Remember, it is a mind game! If Satan has your mind, he has you. I wasted many years and lots of energy in Worry, Fear and Anxiety. It is unrewarded effort and it is a sin. Jesus tells us several times in Matthew 6:25-34 not to worry. *"Therefore I say to you, do not worry about your life, what you will eat or what you will drink; nor about your body, what you will put on. Is not life more than food and the body more than clothing?... Which of you by worrying can add one cubit to his stature? Therefore do not worry about tomorrow, for tomorrow will worry about its own things...*25,27,34(NKJV)

Anxiety almost took over my life. At one point, my doctor prescribed anti-depression and anxiety medication for me after my husband filed for divorce after 33 years of marriage. For over three years, I had been praying for God to fix my marriage, fix me and fix my husband but divorce was never a scenario on how I thought it would end. I felt hurt, heart broken and angry all at the same time. I had no idea what God was doing but I knew I did not like it at all. God was moving things around. He was pruning me for His purpose.

When I allow distractions to come into my relationship with God, my focus is not on Him. When I allow Fear and Anxiety to distract me, I am not trusting God. When I worry, I am not believing that He is the True Sovereign God, Creator and Controller of ALL THINGS, including my life. 1 Chronicles 29:11-12 says, *Everything in the heavens and earth is yours, O Lord, and this is your kingdom. We adore you as being in control of everything. Riches and honor come from you alone, and you are the ruler of all mankind; your hand controls power and might, and it is at your discretion that men are made great and given strength.* (TLB) I have no control BUT I know the One who is in control and I must totally trust in Him. What a "Learning Process" ...to stop climbing on God's throne! To watch God politely waits until I climb down before He moves on my behalf.

I am now Worshipping more and Worrying less.

I am Praising instead of Pondering.

I am Telling my story instead of being Terrified of what others will say.

I am Healing.

I am Thankful.

I am Learning to live like I truly know that God is God!

It has been approximately a two-year journey of regaining my peace. In this new chapter of my life, I am learning to let go of Anxiety and Fear and embrace Peace and Trust.

The Word of God gives life and nourishment to the soul. These prayers from God's Word have helped me make it through some of the most difficult times in my life.

I pray that you allow them to minister to your heart.

Peace and Blessings,

Pam Roberts

PRAYER OF PEACE

LORD God,

You are Jehovah Shalom. You are the God of Peace. You are All-Knowing and You know my deepest fears.

Help me not to fret or have any anxiety about anything, but in every circumstance and in everything, to pray with thanksgiving and make my definite requests known to You.

And God, if I pray this way, Your peace shall be mine. I want to be in that tranquil state of a soul assured of salvation through Christ and fearing nothing from man or God. I want to be content with Your Will being done in heaven, on earth and in my life.

LORD God, I want that peace, which goes beyond all understanding that will break strongholds and build up protectors completely around my heart and mind in Christ Jesus.

And if I focus, O LORD, on what is true, what is worthy of reverence and what is honorable and seemly; on whatever is just, whatever is pure, whatever is lovely and lovable; on whatever is kind and pleasant and gracious.

If there is any virtue and excellence, if there is anything worthy of praise, help me to fix my mind on, meditate on and take into account of all these things.

When I spiritually do what I have learned and what I have received; when I follow what I have heard and what I have seen; when I accept Your Will being done in my life, then Your peace, O God, will be with me.

In Jesus' Name, I Pray,

Amen.

Philippians 4: 6 - 9

Prayer Journal

_____

_____

_____

_____

_____

_____

_____

_____

_____

_____

_____

_____

_____

_____

_____

_____

_____

_____

PRAYER OF TRUST

LORD God,

You are Jehovah Jireh. The LORD will Provide – You completely fulfill and supply my needs. You are my Sustainer and You freely give me nourishment and blessings.

Help me to trust in You more. I want to give You my all. I surrender my life, my heart, my mind and my soul to You.

I do not want to lean on my 'know how' or understanding. My mind is too small and cannot handle or comprehend all that You do and why You do it. I want to acknowledge You, LORD, in all that I do, say and think. When I allow You to lead me, You will guide me in the right direction.

LORD, You are Sovereign and in TOTAL CONTROL of everything in this universe. You orchestrate what happens in my life. When I try to figure things out and be wise in my own eyes, I am not trusting in You. I need to totally surrender to You. I want to trust in You and You alone. I believe, LORD. Help my unbelief.

Help me LORD, to turn away from all things that are not pleasing to You. Change the way I think, the way I act and the things I do. I want to be more like You.

When I trust You and not myself; when I reverence You, LORD, it will be healing to my flesh and strength to my bones. I will be renewed in mind, body and spirit.

I trust You, LORD! I trust You, LORD! I trust You, LORD!

In Jesus' Name, I Pray,

Amen.

Proverbs 3:5-8

Prayer Journal

_____

_____

_____

_____

_____

_____

_____

_____

_____

_____

_____

_____

_____

_____

_____

_____

_____

_____

PRAYER OF LOVE

O LORD, My God,

How Awesome is Your Love. You loved me so much that You sacrificed Your one and only Son for me. And if I believe in Your Son and why He came to earth, I will be granted eternal life.

Heavenly Father, You did not send Your Son to judge and sentence me. You sent Him to save me. All I have to do is BELIEVE, in the name of Jesus, Your Son. If I believe and repent, I will be made innocent through the blood of Jesus. What a great showing of love from You.

Jesus, the Light, came into the world, but we love the darkness instead of the Light. The darkness hides our evil plans and actions. We are afraid of the Light because what evil things we do can be seen.

But God, You see everything I do. What I do in darkness, You see. What I do in the light, You see. I do not want to be with the ones who refuse to trust in You.

Please, guide me. Help me. Show me how to live in the Light. If I live by the truth, LORD, I will come to the Light. I need Your help to live by the truth and to do what You will have me to do.

I want to show the love You have shown me through my actions. I welcome Your Light to work in me, so others can see You in all that I say and do. For Your Glory, LORD. For Your Glory.

In Jesus' Name, I pray,

Amen.

John 3:16-21

Therefore, confess your sins to one another and pray for one another, that you may be healed. The prayer of a righteous person has great power as it is working.

James 5:16 (ESV)

Prayer Journal

_____

_____

_____

_____

_____

_____

_____

_____

_____

_____

_____

_____

_____

_____

_____

_____

PRAYER OF GUIDANCE

LORD God,

You are my Shepherd. You provide everything that I need. Forgive me for allowing my selfish thoughts to think my wants are my needs. Your provisions are sufficient.

Because You, LORD, are my Shepherd, I am dependent on You to lead me and protect me.

You allow me to lie down and rest in green meadows and You lead me beside quite streams.

I must follow You, LORD, because You know what will restore me and gives me new strength.

You guide me in the right direction. If I allow You to show me the way, my actions will honor You and You alone.

When I travel through the valley of trials and tribulations, You LORD give me safe passage. I do not have to be afraid of this dark and rocky place because You are with me every step of the way. Your constant companionship protects me and watches over me.

LORD God, You have prepared a feast for me in the presence of my enemies. I can enjoy being a guest at Your table because You keep my enemies under control.

You, LORD, even anoint me with oil, my blessings from You are overflowing.

I know You are Jehovah Raah (raw-aw') – You are my Shepherd. You are there to comfort me. Now I know for sure that Your goodness, Your love and Your mercy will follow me every day of my life on this earth.

And when this earthly life is over, I will live with You forever in my eternal home.

In Jesus' Name, I Pray,

Amen.

Psalm 23

> And this is the confidence that we have toward him, that if we ask anything according to his will he hears us.
>
> 1 John 5:14 (ESV)

Prayer Journal

_____

_____

_____

_____

_____

_____

_____

_____

_____

_____

_____

_____

_____

_____

_____

_____

PRAYER OF HOPE

LORD, my God.

You are the Most High God. I cry out to You for help, but it seems like You are not listening to me. The situations that are happening in my life, right now, are weighing me down like heavy chains.

The enemy is attacking me from every side. When I feel I am safe, he is waiting for me in ambush ready to drag me away off my designated path. His attacks cause me great pain.

He leaves me helpless and wounded. The pain pierces my heart like an arrow. The ones that are closest to me seem to give me the most heartache.

My strength and my endurance are fading and growing dim. LORD, please remember my suffering and my misery. I feel like I have hit rock bottom.

Satan wants me to feel that You have deserted me and that I have no one to turn to and nowhere to go. BUT, there is one thing, LORD God, that I do remember.

Although my spirit is sad, I HAVE HOPE! It is because of Your mercy and Your loving kindness, LORD.

Your compassion never ceases. Your forgiveness and understanding are new each morning I wake up. When I rise, they are waiting on me.

LORD, You are FAITHFUL TO ME.

LORD, You are FAITHFUL TO ME.

Even when I am not faithful to You, LORD, You are FAITHFUL TO ME! GREAT IS YOUR FAITHFULNESS.

You are my Portion; You are my Inner Being. You, LORD, are my All and All, therefore I HAVE HOPE.

In Jesus' Name, I Pray,

Amen.

Lamentations 3: 8-24

> Be anxious for nothing, but in everything by prayer and supplication, with thanksgiving, let your requests be made known to God;
>
> Philippians 4:6(NKJV)

Prayer Journal

_____

_____

_____

_____

_____

_____

_____

_____

_____

_____

_____

_____

_____

_____

_____

_____

_____

_____

PRAYER OF LIGHT

Great and Might are You, LORD God.

You are my God and I praise Your Holy and Righteous Name.

Your Word tells me that I am the salt of the earth and I am the light of the world.

I believe that You, Lord Jesus, are the One and Only True and Risen Savior. You left Your throne in heaven; came to earth in the form of a baby; and lived as the Ultimate Example for all Christians.

You were mocked, beaten, and crucified and You gave up Your life. You were buried and rose on the third day with ALL POWER!

YOU DID ALL OF THIS FOR ME! JUST FOR ME!

Because I believe in You, Lord, I can be the seasoning that this world is missing. My words can give flavor to someone who does not know You.

My actions can show Your love to someone who has never seen it. As I let my light shine in this world, You shine through me so that others will want to know more about You.

O LORD God, I want everyone who sees me and my actions, give You all the praise, glory and honor. I want them to know that You are God and besides You there is no other god.

No one or nothing can compare to You. No one or nothing can or will ever take Your place.

Holy Spirit, lead me and guide me. Please give me the right words to say. Help me to realize I cannot do this on my own. Open my heart and mind so that I will allow You to be my Teacher and my Guide.

In Jesus' Name, I Pray,

Amen.

Matthew 5:13-16

> rejoicing in hope, patient in tribulation, continuing steadfastly in prayer;
>
> Romans 12:12(NKJV)

Prayer Journal

_____

_____

_____

_____

_____

_____

_____

_____

_____

_____

_____

_____

_____

_____

_____

_____

_____

_____

PRAYER OF STRENGTH

O LORD, my God,

I am weak. My sins are weighing me down. My troubles are like mountains all around me and I cannot seem to find my way.

I need Your strength and I am looking to You to empower me to praise my way through. Forgive me for focusing on my troubles and my sins.

Strengthen me in repentance.

Strengthen me in faith.

When I repent, Your anger turns away from me and You comfort me.

O, my God, I give You honor. I give You praise. You are my salvation. Why am I so afraid? Why do I worry when troubles and trials come in my life? Help me to trust You and not be afraid.

You, Jehovah God, are my strength. You are the song in my heart. You strengthen my soul and You are my salvation. What joy comes over me when I think of Your goodness.

I can now partake from the continuous flow of Your endless joy to deliver me from sin, sorrow and sadness. You, LORD God, are the fountain of goodness to me and I gladly draw out of Your wells of salvation.

I praise You, LORD. I give You glory. You have saved me from me. You are so good to me and I must tell all that I see. Give me holy boldness to tell my story.

Give me power to stand on Your Word. Give me strength and endurance to let the world know You have done great things for me.

I will cry out and let everyone I meet know that You are Great. You are Holy. You are my Strength. You are with me always.

In Jesus' Name, I pray,

Amen.

Isaiah 12

> 'Call on Me, and I will answer you, and show you great and mighty things, which you do not know.'
>
> Jeremiah 33:3(NKJV)

Prayer Journal

_____

_____

_____

_____

_____

_____

_____

_____

_____

_____

_____

_____

_____

_____

_____

_____

_____

_____

PRAYER OF PRAISE

HALLELUJAH! HALLELUJAH!

LORD, I am giving You my highest Praise! I am Your servant, LORD, and I am going to give You all of my Praise.

I must always remember that Your Name is Blessed.

LORD, Your Name is Blessed right now.
LORD, Your Name is Blessed on tomorrow.
LORD, Your Name is Blessed always and forevermore.

When I wake up in the morning, I am going to praise You.
When I lay down at night, I am going to praise You.

Throughout my day, through all my situations, I am going to praise You. Through my trials, I am going to praise You.

LORD, You are higher and greater than anything that has been or will ever be created. Your Glory is higher than all the heavens.

None can measure up to You. You are Majestic.

You are seated high above the earth and the heavens and You look down on me.

You picked me up out of the mess I was in. You rescued me when this world and its people had thrown me away.

 You cleaned me up and now I am Your honored guest.

I must realize that You are aware of my situation and in control of all of my earthly affairs.

You will relieve my suffering in Your time and not mine.

You will not let me to perish, so I will praise You, LORD, while I wait on You.

I give You the highest praise.

HALLELUJAH!! HALLELUJAH!!

In Jesus' Name, I pray,

Amen.

Psalm 113

> LORD, I cry out to You; Make haste to me! Give ear to my voice when I cry out to You. Let my prayer be set before You as incense, the lifting up of my hand as the evening sacrifice.
>
> Psalm 141:1-2(NKJV)

Prayer Journal

_____

_____

_____

_____

_____

_____

_____

_____

_____

_____

_____

_____

_____

_____

_____

_____

_____

PRAYER OF SPIRITUAL WISDOM

LORD God, my heavenly Father,

ALL PRAISES go to You, the Father of my Lord and Savior, Jesus Christ. You chose me before the creation of this world to be holy and blameless. You, LORD God, preordained my adoption through Jesus Christ in accordance to Your pleasure and will.

I have been redeemed through the blood of Jesus Christ. LORD God, I am forgiven of sins because of the unrestrained and extravagant richness of Your Grace given to me with all wisdom and understanding.

God, we were chosen to belong to You. Everything works in conformity with the purpose of Your will. We put our hope in Christ and we were chosen to bring praise to Your glory.

I am now included in Christ because I heard the Word of Truth, the Gospel of my salvation and trusted in Him. LORD God, I am now Your possession. I am marked with the seal of the Holy Spirit. I am guaranteed my inheritance.

Heavenly Father, I am asking You to give me the Spirit of wisdom and revelation.

I want to know You better, LORD God.

I want to know You better, Jesus.

I want to know You better, Holy Spirit.

I need each of You in my life. You are ALL special to me.

I want You to enlighten the eyes of my heart so that I may understand the confident hope that You have given me. I want to know the riches of Your glorious inheritance.

I want to know LORD God, Your incomparable great power because I believe. The same power that raised Jesus Christ from the dead. The same power that has seated Him in the place of honor at Your right hand in Heaven. The same power that is above all that rules with authority, power and dominion, and every title that was given in the past, present and will be given in the future.

I need to always realize, LORD God, that You are in TOTAL CONTROL. You put all things under the authority of Your Son, Jesus Christ. You made Him Head over all things for the benefit of the church.

You, LORD God, made the church the body of Christ and it is made full and complete by Christ Who fills everything in every way with Himself.

In Jesus' Name, I pray,

Amen.

Ephesians 1: 4-23

The LORD is far from the wicked, but he hears the prayer of the righteous.

Proverbs 15:29(ESV)

Prayer Journal

_____

_____

_____

_____

_____

_____

_____

_____

_____

_____

_____

_____

_____

_____

_____

_____

_____

_____

_____

PRAYER OF ADORATION
(STEADFAST LOVE)

To the One and Only True God.

Creator and Ruler of the Universe and of my life, I GIVE YOU PRAISE!

I give thanks to You, O LORD, because You are good and Your mercy is everlasting.

I give thanks to the God above all other gods. Your compassion is endless.

I give thanks to You, LORD of lords. Your mercy is everlasting.

I give thanks to the One who alone can do great miracles and wonders. Your faithful love never fails.

You LORD God made the heavens by Your wisdom. Your mercy is everlasting.

You are the architect of the earth over the waters. Your mercy is everlasting.

You made the great and awesome lights in the sky. Your mercy is everlasting.

You created the sun to rule the day and the moon to rule the night. Your mercy is everlasting.

You, O LORD, have always taken care of Your people. It is Your hand that saves me when trouble comes.

You struck down Egypt by killing their first born. You brought the children of Israel out of Egypt's bondage. Your mercy is everlasting.

With a strong hand and an outstretched arm, You divided the Red Sea and allowed Israel to pass though on dry land. Your mercy is everlasting.

You led Your people through the wilderness. Your mercy is everlasting.

You struck down great and famous kings. Si'hon, king of the Amorites and Og, king of Bashan were destroyed. Your mercy is everlasting.

You gave Your servants Israel the land of their enemies. Your mercy is everlasting.

LORD, my God, You are the One who remembered me when trouble and trials were weighing me down. For Your mercy is everlasting!

You rescued me from my enemies and from the storms that raged in my life. Your mercy is everlasting!

You are Provider and Sustainer of all. Your mercy is everlasting!

I give thanks to my God. The Creator and Ruler of the heavens and the earth. For Your mercy and love is everlasting!

In Jesus' Name, I pray,

Amen.

Psalm 136

> But when you ask, you must believe. You must not doubt. That's because person who doubts is like a wave of the sea. The wind blows and tosses them around.
>
> James 1:6(NIRV)

Prayer Journal

_____

_____

_____

_____

_____

_____

_____

_____

_____

_____

_____

_____

_____

_____

_____

_____

PRAYER OF REPENTANCE

LORD Jehovah,

Have mercy on me, O God, according to Your lovingkindness. Show me favor, O LORD, according to Your abundance of tender mercy.

Blot out all of my wrong doings. Wash me thoroughly from my wickedness.

Please LORD, make me clean from my sin and my guilt. I know the sinful things I have done are always before me.

I have sinned against You LORD, and only You. I have done evil in Your sight. You have every right to sentence me harshly for my actions. Your judgment is fair.

I have been a sinner since I was born. I know that I have been this way since my conception.

You, LORD, desire and deserve honesty from my heart. You want utter sincerity and truthfulness from the inner most part of me.

Indwell me and be permanently present in my heart. Teach me and give me Your wisdom.

Clean me thoroughly with hyssop. Make me pure. Wash me, LORD, and I shall be whiter than snow.

Please take away all of my sins and blot out the evil I have done.

I want to be forgiven. Create in me a clean heart, O God, and renew in me a spirit that is faithful and pleasing to You.

LORD, do not throw me away or banish me from Your presence. Do not take Your Holy Spirit from me.

I want the joy of Your salvation restored to me and give me a willing spirit to obey You.

In Jesus' Name, I Pray,

Amen.

Psalm 51:1-12

> In my distress I called upon the LORD, And cried out to my God; He heard my voice from His temple, And my cry came before Him, even to His ears.
>
> Psalm 18:6(NKJV)

Prayer Journal

_____

_____

_____

_____

_____

_____

_____

_____

_____

_____

_____

_____

_____

_____

_____

_____

_____

_____

PRAYER OF EVANGELISM

O LORD God, my God,

Great is Your faithfulness. You are Creator and Ruler of this universe and I give You Praise.

Each day, LORD, please help me to know in my heart that Christ Jesus is my Lord and Savior.

I want to always be ready to give a response to anyone who asks me about the hope I have in You. I want my response to be gentle and respectful to all I come in contact with.

Let my way of living be an example of You, Lord Jesus. Let my conduct and words in public, as well as in private, show that I am a believer of Jesus Christ, my Savior.

Help me, LORD, to stand strong and be faithful to You when people say evil things about how I am living for You. Let them be put to shame for speaking against You, O LORD.

Help me not to worry about my feelings or being hurt for doing what is right according to Your Word. O God, I want to do what pleases You and only You.

In Jesus' Name, I Pray,

Amen.

I Peter 3:15-17

> So Peter was kept in prison, but earnest prayer for him was made to God by the church.
>
> Acts 12:5(ESV)

Prayer Journal

_____

_____

_____

_____

_____

_____

_____

_____

_____

_____

_____

_____

_____

_____

_____

_____

_____

PRAYER OF HARVEST

LORD GOD,

You are All-seeing and All-knowing. You know what I am going to say before I think it. I give You glory and honor for being God.

Give me the right words to speak and the right time to speak them. Let the words I speak not return to me without producing results.

I want my words to accomplish their purpose and do exactly what I send them to do. After I have spoken to Your people, let them leave my presence with Your Joy and Your Peace. (Isaiah 55:11-12)

Give me holy boldness, Holy Spirit. You are my Helper and my Guide. Please indwell me so that I can be the Lord's witness wherever I go, without fear. Give me the power to walk and speak by faith at home, at work, in my neighborhood, city, state, country and world. (Acts 1:8)

LORD, You loved me so much that You gave Your Only Son to die so that I could be saved. Your promise is that whosoever believes in the purpose of Jesus Christ for coming to earth would not perish but have everlasting life.

You wanted all of my sins forgiven through Your Son, Jesus Christ. You wanted me to be Your heir and for You to be my God.

I am Your instrument. Use me, LORD, to go to Your people to open their eyes and turn them from darkness to light. Use me LORD, to turn Your people from Satan's power to Your power. Lead me, Holy Spirit, when to speak and when to listen. Give me the right words to say to Your people. (Acts 26:16-18)

LORD God, let me not lose faith or be discouraged. Give me endurance, patience, and long suffering needed to tell others about Christ. (Luke 22:32)

In Jesus' Name, I pray,

Amen.

Hear me when I call, O God of my righteousness! You have relieved me in my distress; Have mercy on me, and hear my prayer.   Psalm 4:1(NKJV)

Prayer Journal

_____

_____

_____

_____

_____

_____

_____

_____

_____

_____

_____

_____

_____

_____

_____

_____

_____

_____

PRAYER OF HUMBLE INCREASE

My Heavenly Father,

You are All Powerful, All Seeing and All Knowing.

You are my Provider and Sustainer.

Please wash me in the blood of the Lamb and forgive me of all my sins before I make my requests known to You.

LORD, I am Your servant. I am depending on You to help me. I am depending on You to bless me.

I want Your Hand to lead me, protect me and strengthen me. Please, LORD, lead me on my job (in my business). Give me the right words to say so that You can meet my employer's needs (my client's needs) through me.

Let Your will be done in my life. Give me acceptance of Your will because You are in total control.

Remind me daily that my thoughts are not Your thoughts; that my ways are not Your ways; that Your perfect timing is not on my worldly schedule.

Enlarge my love for You.

Prosper my endeavors.

Enlarge my territory and my finances so that I may be able to give my best back to You.

Keep me from evil and discouragement that I may not cause myself or my family needless pain or grief.

I want to live a life pleasing to You.

I am waiting on You with great expectation and I will forever give You all the Praise, all the Glory and all the Honor.

In Jesus' Name, I Pray,

Amen.

I Chronicles 4:10

Isaiah 55:9-10

> Now it came to pass in those days that He went out to the mountain to pray, and continued all night in prayer to God.
>
> Luke 6:12(NKJV)

Prayer Journal

_____

_____

_____

_____

_____

_____

_____

_____

_____

_____

_____

_____

_____

_____

_____

_____

_____

_____

PRAYER OF POWER AND PRESENCE

LORD God,

You are Omnipotent and Omnipresent. Your power reigns throughout this universe and in my life.

LORD God, You know me. I can hide nothing from You because You know everything there is to know about me. You have searched me and know what is in my heart.

You know me by name, LORD. You know when I sit down and when I get up. You are in heaven and I am here on earth and You still know exactly what I am thinking before I think it.

You are everywhere at the same time. You know when I am in school, at work or at home because You are already there. You know exactly what I am going to do before I do it.

You know I am lying, when others think I am telling the truth. You know I am being disobedient when no one else sees me.

LORD, You even know what I am going to say before I say it. Your Power is awesome and amazing!

You are all around me. You are in front of me, behind me, over me and under me. You hold me safe in Your hands. You know me so well, it just amazes me. It is too much for me to understand.

You are Worthy and I give You all the Glory and Honor.

In Jesus' Name, I pray,

Amen.

Psalm 139:1-6

...a message came to him from the LORD. He said, "Go back and speak to Hezekiah. He is the ruler of my people. Tell him 'The LORD, the God of King David, says, "I have heard your prayer. I have seen your tears. And I will heal you..."'"

2 Kings 20:4-5(NIRV)

Prayer Journal

_____

_____

_____

_____

_____

_____

_____

_____

_____

_____

_____

_____

_____

_____

_____

_____

_____

_____

PRAYER OF WORSHIP

O LORD, my LORD,
How excellent is Your name in all the earth,
Who have set Your glory above the heavens! [Psalm 8:1]

Give unto the LORD the glory due to His name;
Worship the LORD in the beauty of holiness. [Psalm 29:2]

Bless the LORD, O my soul;
And all that is within me, bless His holy name! [Psalm 103:1]

Let them praise the name of the LORD,
For His name alone is exalted;
His glory is above the earth and heaven. [Psalm 148:13]

You, O LORD, are worthy of my absolute worship and devotion because….

You are El Shaddai (el shad-di') – The LORD God Almighty, the All-Sufficient One. You freely give Your nourishment and blessing to me. You are my Sustainer.

You are El Elyon (el el-yone') – The Most High God. You are the Absolute Ruler of All. You are Sovereign. Everything in the heavens and earth is Yours, O LORD, and this is Your kingdom. I adore You as being in control of everything.

You are El Olam (el o-lawm') – The Everlasting God. You are the LORD and Creator of the ends of the earth. You never get tired or weary. You are Alpha and Omega, the Beginning and the End, the First and the Last.

You are Yahweh (yah-weh) – LORD, Jehovah. You are Master and LORD. You are Omnipotent, possessing All Power. There is none like You.

You are Jehovah Nisse (nis-see') – You LORD are my Banner, my Miracle and my Refuge. You go before me and You are my Hope and my Focal Point. You are my Protection and my Place of Safety.

You are Jehovah Raah (raw-aw') – You LORD are my Shepherd and I am Your sheep. Your rod and staff comfort me. I know that You provide and care for me. I cannot survive without You. You, LORD, continuously restore me and lead me.

You are Jehovah Rapha (raw-faw') – You LORD are my Healer. You are the Great Physician who heals me physically, spiritually and emotionally.

You are Jehovah Shammah (shawm'maw) – You LORD are always there. You are Omnipresent. You are everywhere at the same time. There is no place I can go that You are not already there.

You are Jehovah Jireh (yir-eh') – You LORD are my Provider. You supply for me all that I need physically and spiritually. I depend on You for everything.

You are Jehovah Shalom (shaw-lome') – You LORD are my Peace. I can lie down in peace and sleep. I can walk daily in peace, Your Great Peace, not the peace that the world gives, but that which only You can give.

I worship You and will forever give You All the Praise, Glory and Honor.

In Jesus' Name, I pray,

Amen.

> The LORD is righteous in all his ways and kind in all his works.
> The LORD is near to all who call on him, to all who call on him in truth.
>
> Psalm 145:17-18(ESV)

Prayer Journal

_____

_____

_____

_____

_____

_____

_____

_____

_____

_____

_____

_____

_____

_____

_____

_____

_____

_____

PRAYER OF WARFARE

Awesome and Powerful God.

You are Mighty in battle. You are Holy and I worship You. I am depending on Your power for strength.

Satan has been against You, LORD, since the beginning of time and he wants to use me to get to You. I am fighting in a war to the death for my mind and my soul.

LORD, I am a soldier in Your army. I need Your spiritual strength and courage to fight in this spiritual war. Help me to put on all the armor each day. I must keep it on at all times to fight against the temptations of my flesh.

When I am mistreated by my loved ones;

When manipulators and fast talkers try to influence me;

When my spouse discourages me;

When my children are disobedient;

When anxiety creeps in;

When things at my job are not going well;

When doubt fills my mind;

I must remember LORD that this is spiritual warfare, not physical hand to hand combat. I am not fighting against flesh and blood. I am fighting against spiritual wickedness in high places. I want to be able to stand firm no matter what evil or problem is pressing against me.

LORD, help me to put the *Belt of Truth* around my waist. Your truth hold up the rest of my armor. Your Truth encourages me daily.

LORD, help me to put on the *Breastplate of Righteousness*. Being right with You strengthens my heart for war and keeps my heart protected in battle.

LORD, help me to cover my feet with the preparation of the *Gospel of Peace*. Clear knowledge of Your Word keeps me moving forward in battle no matter how rough the battle gets. Your Word keeps me planted.

LORD, help me to pick up and hold fast to the *Shield of Faith* so I am able to extinguish any flaming arrows of doubt and fear the enemy throws at me. Without faith, it is impossible to please You.

LORD, help me to put on the *Helmet of Salvation*. You saved me through the blood of Christ Jesus, Your Son. My hope in You keeps my mind on You and off of my problems.

LORD, help me to pick up the *Sword of the Spirit*; Your Word, my weapon every day. Your Word has power to build me up and make the enemy flee. Help me to apply Your Word to every situation in my life.

Now that I am dressed for battle, I must bond all of my armor with prayer, so I can be an effective soldier. LORD, teach me how to pray and what to pray for. Help me to endure. Strengthen me and my fellow soldiers.

Holy Spirit guide me. LORD, keep me alert and watchful. Never let me take off any of my armor or put my weapon down for any reason.

Help me to STAND FAST until the end.

In Jesus' Name, I pray,

Amen.

Ephesians 6:11-18

> Give ear to my words, O LORD; Consider my meditation. Give heed to the voice of my cry, My King and my God, for to You I will pray. My voice You shall hear in the morning, O LORD; In the morning I will direct it to You, And I will look up.
>
> Psalm 5:1-3(NKJV)

Prayer Journal

_____

_____

_____

_____

_____

_____

_____

_____

_____

_____

_____

_____

_____

_____

_____

_____

_____

_____

PRAYER OF TRIUMPH AND REJOICING

LORD God,

You are Omnipotent and Sovereign. I have heard and read of the great things about You. I have seen Your works in my life.

You deserve my worship and my respect. Your great and mighty acts should bring me to my knees each time I think about You and what You have done for me and for others.

I am asking You, O LORD, to work in my life, just as You have done before.

When You look at my life and determine what I need, please LORD, have mercy on me. Help me realize that You love me in spite of my sins, my trials and my situation. You know what is best for me.

LORD, You are Creator, Ruler, and Controller of ALL THINGS. Your Glory covers the Heavens. The earth is full of Your Praise.

Your brightness was like the light. Rays flashed from Your hand and there was the hiding place of Your Power.

Before You, went pestilence and plague followed at Your feet.

You stood and measured the earth. You looked around and nations trembled. The mountains scattered and the hills fell down low.

You divided the earth with rivers. The sun and the moon stood still at Your command.

You marched through in fury and crushed evil nations in anger. You crushed the head of the house of the wicked. You destroyed those who came to destroy Your people.

O, MY GOD. YOUR RECORD IS GOOD!!

Although fear from my situations and my impatience overtakes me at times, I MUST WAIT ON YOU AND REJOICE!

If the fig tree does not bud; when there is no fruit on the vines.

If the olive crop fails and the field produces not food.

When the flock is cut off and there is no herd in the stalls.

When my body is sick and in pain.

When my family member(s) are not following Your Word;

When I am jobless and homeless.

When I feel like the walls of life are closing in on me;

Yet will I REJOICE in You, O LORD. I will take JOY in the God of my salvation.

You are my strength. You will provide ALL that I need to endure until You determine the right time for my trials to be over.

Strengthen me, LORD, and make my steps sturdy so that I can walk spiritually higher in each circumstance in my life. I want to keep Your Joy on the Journey.

In Jesus' Name, I pray,
Amen.

Habakkuk 3

For the eyes of the Lord are on the righteous, and his ears are open to their prayer. But the face of the Lord is against those who do evil.

1 Peter 3:12(ESV)

Prayer Journal

_____

_____

_____

_____

_____

_____

_____

_____

_____

_____

_____

_____

_____

_____

_____

_____

_____

_____

_____

PRAYER OF PROTECTION

LORD, my GOD,

You are Creator and Ruler of this universe. You are the Creator of ALL things. I worship You for Who You are.

I am struggling, LORD. I am trying to keep my mind on You and Your love. Problems in my life are weighing me down and I feel that I am buckling under the pressure.

But Your Word says that if I rest in the shadow of the Most High God, I will be kept safe by the Mighty One. That is YOU! You will keep me safe.

You, LORD, are my Place of Safety. You are like a fort to me. I run to You when trouble and danger are pursuing me. You are my God and I trust in You.

I will not walk in fear because You will surely save me from Satan's hidden traps and from deadly sickness. This does not mean that I will not get sick or have bodily difficulties, but that You will be with me because You cover me with Your wings.

You are faithful to me and under Your feathers I will find safety like a shield or a tower.

LORD God, Your Word is my shield and my protection. I do not have to be afraid of terrors that come to me during the nights of my life.

I will not be afraid of the arrows that are directed to me during the days of my life.

I do not have to be afraid of plagues that walk in the dark times of my life.

I will not be afraid of anything making my life so unrepairable that You, LORD God cannot fix. Thank You, LORD, for Your promises!

You assure me that danger will come close to me. The devastation will be so close I could reach out and touch it but no harm will come to me.

You are right there controlling the situation and working it out for my good. My God, You will let me see with my eyes how You punish the sinful people around me who mean to do me harm.

If I acknowledge that You LORD are the One who keeps me safe; if I let the Most High God be like a home to me; if I commune with You, then no harm will come to me. No disease or outbreak will even come near my dwelling place.

You will dispatch Your angels to take good care of me. Your angels will lift me up in their hands and I will not even trip over stumbling blocks in my life. What Awesome Power!!

I will walk through great trials and tribulations and with Your power, I will be able to crush them and come out victorious.

You will save the one who loves You and calls You by name. You are the true Omnipotent One; the one and only reigning, living God. You promised to keep me safe, because of my love for You and my trust in You.

When I call, You will answer me. Troubles will come, but You will be with me every step of the way. You are going to save me and keep me righteous.

You are going to give me a satisfied life through Your salvation. I cannot make it without You.

I LOVE YOU LORD!

I TRUST YOU LORD!

I NEED YOU LORD!

In Jesus' Name, I pray,

Amen. Amen. Amen!

Psalm 91

This poor man cried, and the LORD heard him, and saved him out of all his troubles.

Psalm 34:6 (KJV)

Prayer Journal

_____

_____

_____

_____

_____

_____

_____

_____

_____

_____

_____

_____

_____

_____

_____

_____

_____

_____

PRAYER OF SPIRITUAL GROWTH

LORD God, my Heavenly Father.

You are Powerful and Glorious. When I think of Your Sovereignty and Awesomeness, I fall to my knees in reverence of You.

You are the Creator and Ruler of all! You control everything in the heavens and on earth. You know, LORD, what is best for me.

You left Your Holy Spirit here to be my Teacher and my Guide. He is always willing to help me if I invite Him into every situation of my life.

I am asking You Heavenly Father, to strengthen me spiritually from Your glorious and unlimited resources. I want the power of Your Holy Spirit to be permanently present in the inner most part of me so that my heart can be spiritually cultivated to be planted with Your Word.

When I open up that inner most part of me and feast on Your Word; when I trust in You completely, then Christ, my Savior, will make my heart His home.

As Your Word indwells me, my spiritual roots will grow strong and deep into God's love. This will keep me strong in You, Lord.

Please grant me the power to understand how extreme Your love is for me. All of Your chosen people need to know how wide and how long and how high and how deep Your love is for each of us.

I want to experience the love of Christ that is so massive it cannot be fully comprehended. I want to be made complete with all the fullness of life and power that comes from You, my Heavenly Father.

Now unto You, LORD God, Who is all powerful and all knowing, I give You glory as Creator and Ruler of all things. Through Your Power that works within me to accomplish infinitely more that I can ask or imagine.

I give all glory to You, in the church and in Christ Jesus through all generations forever and ever.

In Jesus' Name I Pray,

Amen.

Ephesians 3:14-21

In this manner, therefore, pray:

Our Father in heaven, Hallowed be Your name.

Your kingdom come. Your will be done on earth as it is in heaven.

Give us this day our daily bread. And forgive us our debts, as we forgive our debtors. And do not lead us into temptation,

But deliver us from the evil one. For Yours is the kingdom and the power and the glory forever. Amen.

Matthew 6:9-13(NKJV)

Prayer Journal

_____

_____

_____

_____

_____

_____

_____

_____

_____

_____

_____

_____

_____

_____

_____

SINNER'S PRAYER

LORD God,

I am a sinner and I need Your forgiveness. I have done things that were wrong and not pleasing to You. Your word says that if I confess with my mouth that Jesus is Lord and if I believe in my heart that You, God raised Him from the dead, I will be saved.

So right now, LORD God, I declare and accept that Jesus is Lord. I recognize and believe that You, the One and Only All Powerful God, raised Him from the dead. I am now SAVED!

Thank You God for the gift of salvation. In my heart, I am now made right with You. There is nothing in my life that is so bad that it is not covered by the blood of Jesus Christ, our Lord. I can now tell others that I believe. I can tell others that You saved me. I now have an eternal home in heaven with You when I die and leave this earthly place.

Thank You, God for sending Your Son, Jesus, to pay the penalty for my sins, past, present and future.

In Jesus' Name, I pray,

Amen.

Romans 10:9-10

> Then you will call upon me and come and pray to me, and I will hear you. You will seek me and find me, when you seek me with all your heart.
>
> Jeremiah 29:12-13(ESV)

Prayer Journal

_____

_____

_____

_____

_____

_____

_____

_____

_____

_____

_____

_____

_____

_____

_____

_____

_____

_____

67850390R00042

Made in the USA
Lexington, KY
23 September 2017